EARTH'S ENERGY EXPERIMENTS

WATER ENERGY PROJECTS

Easy Energy Activities for
Future Engineers!

MEGAN BORGERT-SPANIOL

CONSULTING EDITOR, DIANE CRAIG, M.A./READING SPECIALIST

Super Sandcastle

An Imprint of Abdo Publishing
abdopublishing.com

abdopublishing.com

Published by Abdo Publishing, a division of ABDO, PO Box 398166, Minneapolis, Minnesota 55439. Copyright © 2019 by Abdo Consulting Group, Inc. International copyrights reserved in all countries. No part of this book may be reproduced in any form without written permission from the publisher. Super SandCastle™ is a trademark and logo of Abdo Publishing.

Printed in the United States of America, North Mankato, Minnesota
052018
092018

Design and Production: Mighty Media, Inc.
Editor: Liz Salzmann
Cover Photographs: Mighty Media, Inc.; Shutterstock
Interior Photographs: iStockphoto; Mighty Media, Inc.; Shutterstock; Wikimedia Commons

The following manufacturers/names appearing in this book are trademarks:
Artist's Loft™, Pyrex®, Sharpie®

Library of Congress Control Number: 2017961712

Publisher's Cataloging-in-Publication Data
Names: Borgert-Spaniol, Megan, author.
Title: Water energy projects: Easy energy activities for future engineers! / by Megan Borgert-Spaniol.
Other titles: Easy energy activities for future engineers!
Description: Minneapolis, Minnesota : Abdo Publishing, 2019. | Series: Earth's energy experiments
Identifiers: ISBN 9781532115660 (lib.bdg.) | ISBN 9781532156380 (ebook)
Subjects: LCSH: Water-power--Juvenile literature. | Handicraft--Juvenile literature. | Science projects--Juvenile literature. | Water--Experiments--Juvenile literature.
Classification: DDC 333.914--dc23

Super SandCastle™ books are created by a team of professional educators, reading specialists, and content developers around five essential components—phonemic awareness, phonics, vocabulary, text comprehension, and fluency—to assist young readers as they develop reading skills and strategies and increase their general knowledge. All books are written, reviewed, and leveled for guided reading and early reading intervention programs for use in shared, guided, and independent reading and writing activities to support a balanced approach to literacy instruction.

TO ADULT HELPERS

The projects in this title are fun and simple. There are just a few things to remember to keep kids safe. Some projects require the use of sharp or hot objects. Also, kids may be using messy materials such as glue or paint. Make sure they protect their clothes and work surfaces. Review the projects before starting, and be ready to assist when necessary.

KEY SYMBOLS

Watch for these warning symbols in this book. Here is what they mean.

HOT!
You will be working with something hot. Get help!

SHARP!
You will be working with a sharp object. Get help!

CONTENTS

WHAT IS WATER ENERGY?

Water energy is power gained from water when it's in motion. People can direct the force of water. Then they use the energy in different ways.

WATER ENERGY

Water energy is often used to create electricity. Electricity made this way is called hydroelectricity. It powers homes, businesses, and more!

Water energy is a renewable **resource**. This is because water doesn't get used up. The world is unlikely to run out of it.

HOOVER DAM WATER POWER PLANT

Hydroelectricity is a type of clean power. Producing it does not pollute the air. It also costs less than most other types of power. Users pay less for power when it comes from water energy. Today, water energy produces about 7 percent of the electricity in the United States.

INSIDE A WATER POWER PLANT

WATER POWER PLANTS

There are three types of water power plants. All types use **turbines** and **generators** to produce electricity. But each uses a different method to capture the energy of the water.

IMPOUNDMENT PLANT

Impoundment plants are the most common type of water power plant. They use dams to collect water in **reservoirs**. This water flows through turbines, causing them to turn. The turbines run generators that create electricity. Power lines carry the electricity from the plant to homes and businesses.

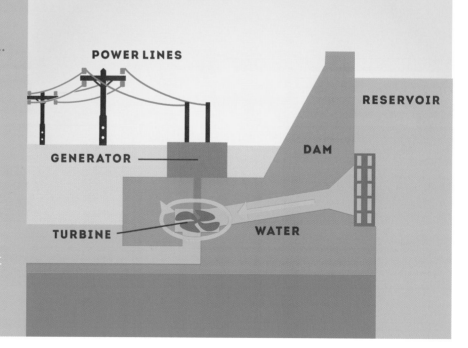

POWER LINES

RESERVOIR

GENERATOR

DAM

TURBINE

WATER

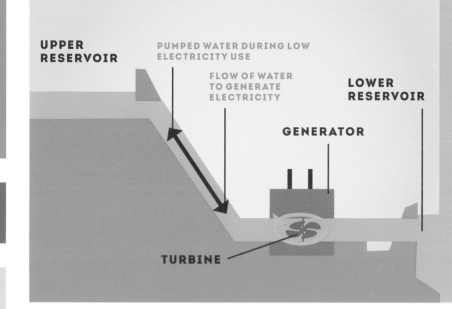

UPPER RESERVOIR

PUMPED WATER DURING LOW ELECTRICITY USE

FLOW OF WATER TO GENERATE ELECTRICITY

LOWER RESERVOIR

GENERATOR

TURBINE

PUMPED STORAGE PLANT

A pumped storage plant uses two **reservoirs**. Water flows from an upper reservoir through a **turbine**. That water is stored in a lower reservoir. When electricity use is low, water is pumped to the upper reservoir. When electricity use is high, water is released again through the turbine.

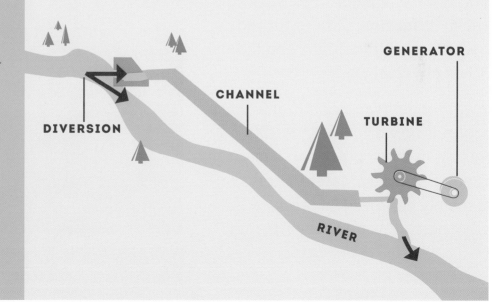

DIVERSION PLANT

A **diversion** plant captures the energy of a river's natural flow. Part of a river is diverted into a channel. The channel directs the water to a turbine.

DIVERSION

CHANNEL

GENERATOR

TURBINE

RIVER

WATER ENERGY HISTORY

Humans have been using water energy for thousands of years. The ancient Egyptians. Greeks, and Romans all built waterwheels on the edges of rivers.

Some waterwheels lifted water for use in **irrigation**. Others turned mills that ground grains and did other **physical** work.

Waterwheels were commonly used around the world until the 1800s. People in some places still use them. But today, water energy is mainly captured to produce electricity at water power plants.

OLD ROMAN WATERWHEELS IN SYRIA

LESTER ALLAN PELTON

Lester Allan Pelton was an American inventor. In the 1850s, he observed the waterwheels miners used. He noticed a lot of the water's energy was wasted. In the 1870s, Pelton invented a waterwheel with divided cups. This used more of the water's energy. Water power plants today still use wheels similar to Pelton's!

PELTON-STYLE TURBINE WHEEL

WATERWHEEL ENERGY

When water hits a single cup, it splashes up. The water's force presses only in the middle of the cup. And the force stops when the water splashes up. The water's energy isn't applied to the whole cup.

When water hits the divider of a Pelton cup, it flows out each side. The water's force presses along the entire cup. So, more energy is applied to the cup.

TURBINE WHEEL   **SINGLE CUP**   **PELTON CUP**

MATERIALS

Here are some of the materials that you will need for the projects in this book.

CORK

CRAFT FOAM

CRAFT STICKS

DRINKING STRAWS

DUCT TAPE

FOOD COLORING

FUNNEL

HAMMER

HOLE PUNCH

HOT GLUE GUN & GLUE STICKS

LIQUID MEASURING CUP

METAL WASHERS

NAIL

PAINT PENS

PITCHER

PLASTIC BOTTLE

PLASTIC CUP

PLASTIC JAR

PLASTIC LID

PLASTIC WRAP

PUSHPINS

RUBBER BAND

STRING

STYROFOAM CUP

WOODEN SKEWERS

WATER CYCLE IN A JAR

MATERIALS: empty plastic jar, black marker, paint pens, liquid measuring cup, water, blue food coloring, spoon, funnel, plastic wrap, rubber band

The water **cycle** is a natural process that Earth's water supply goes through. Throughout this cycle, water changes from a liquid to a gas and back to a liquid or a solid. The water cycle repeats itself continuously. Water is not used up in the process. It just changes states. This is why water is a renewable source of energy!

1 Use black marker and paint pens to draw the sun, a cloud, and ocean waves on the jar.

2 Draw an arrow from the ocean to the sun. Label the arrow "**evaporation**."

3 Write "**condensation**" inside the cloud,

4 Draw dotted lines from the cloud to the ocean. Label them "**precipitation**."

5 Fill the measuring cup with water. Stir in two drops of blue food coloring.

Continued on the next page.

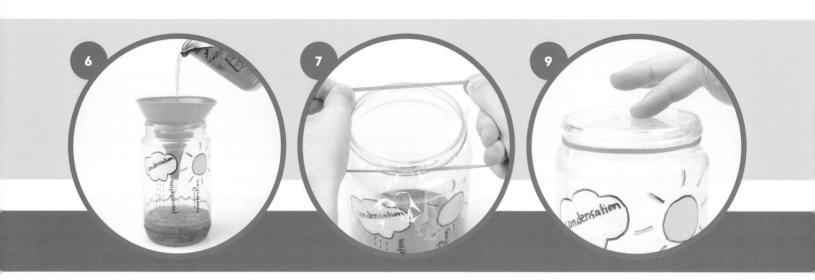

6 Set the funnel in the jar's opening. Pour the blue water into the jar until the jar is about one-fourth full.

7 Cover the top of the jar with plastic wrap. Use a rubber band to seal the wrap tightly.

8 Place the jar near a sunny window. Leave the jar in the sun for several hours.

9 Watch for water droplets to form inside the jar. Then observe the jar. Lightly tap the plastic wrap to make the water droplets fall. Do you see the water **cycle** at work?

DIGGING DEEPER

The water **cycle** has three main **phases**. They are **evaporation**, **condensation**, and **precipitation**. Heat from the sun warms Earth's bodies of water. This causes water to evaporate into a gas called water vapor. Water vapor cools as it rises into the sky. This makes it condense into tiny droplets. These droplets form clouds. Some droplets become too heavy to stay in the air. The droplets fall back to Earth as precipitation. This precipitation can be a liquid, such as rain, or a frozen solid, such as snow or hail.

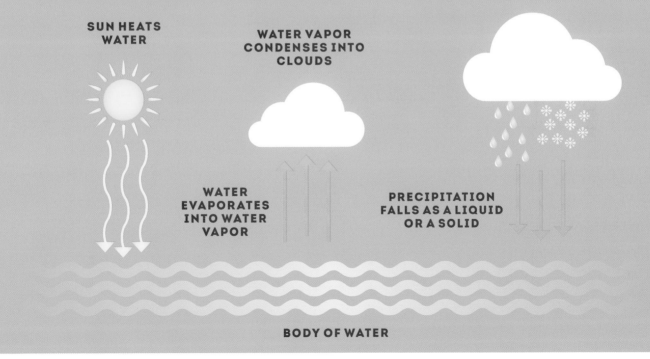

SUN HEATS WATER

WATER VAPOR CONDENSES INTO CLOUDS

WATER EVAPORATES INTO WATER VAPOR

PRECIPITATION FALLS AS A LIQUID OR A SOLID

BODY OF WATER

WATER TURBINE IN A BOTTLE

MATERIALS: empty 1-liter water bottle, scissors, ruler, marker, pushpin, pencil, 2 drinking straws, duct tape, hole punch, string, pitcher, water, large tub (optional)

Water power plants change the water flow depending on how much electricity is needed. When use is high, more water is released to flow through the **turbines**. This makes the turbines turn faster, which creates more electricity.

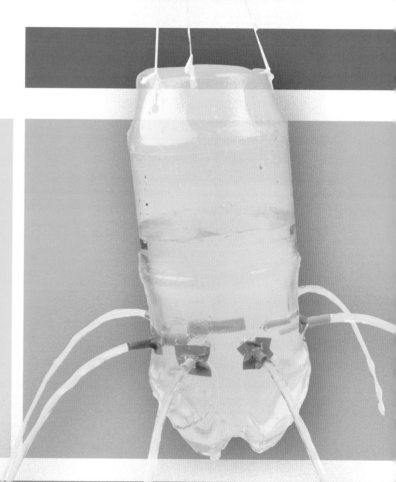

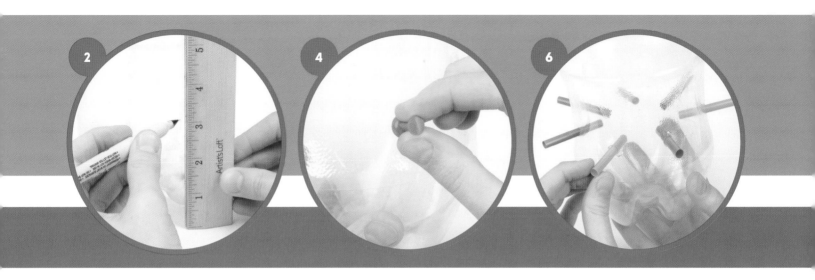

① Cut the top off the plastic bottle.

② Hold a ruler next to the bottle. Make a dot on the bottle 3 inches (7.5 cm) from the bottom.

③ Repeat step 2 to make seven more dots around the base of the bottle.

④ Use a pushpin to poke a hole at each dot. Use a pencil to make the holes bigger.

⑤ Cut each straw into four equal pieces.

⑥ Push a straw piece into each of the holes in the bottle.

Continued on the next page.

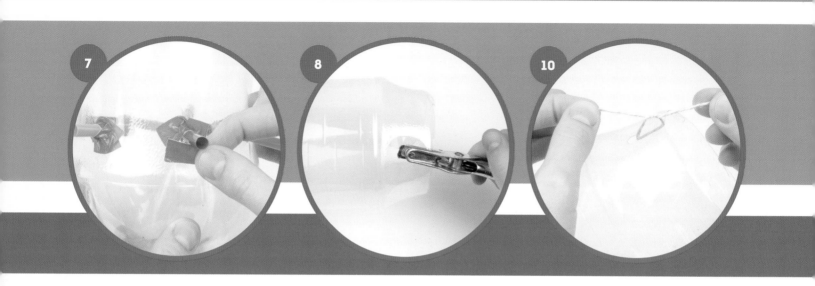

7 Put tape around each straw to seal any cracks.

8 Use a hole punch to make three holes near the top of the bottle. Space them evenly around the bottle.

9 Cut four pieces of string. Make them each 12 inches (30 cm) long.

10 Tie a piece of string through each of the three holes.

11 Tie the other ends of the three strings together in a knot.

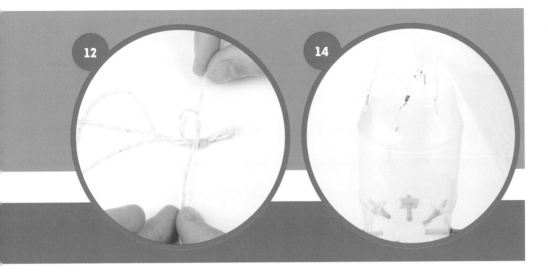

12 Tie the fourth string around the knot.

13 Fill the pitcher with water. Bring the bottle outdoors or hold it over a tub.

14 Hold the bottle by the fourth string. Slowly pour water into the bottle.

15 Watch as the water makes the bottle spin! Try filling the bottle halfway with water. Then fill it to the top. Does this affect how fast the bottle spins?

DIGGING DEEPER

In this experiment, the bottle represents a **turbine**. Water flows through the straws with greater force when the bottle is full. This makes the bottle spin faster.

Similarly, turbines spin faster when more water is released into them. This creates more electricity. A water power plant can control the flow of water to the turbines. That is one way a plant controls the amount of electricity it produces.

CORK-AND-BOTTLE WATER MILL

MATERIALS: hammer, nail, cork, wooden skewer, small plastic cup, scissors, duct tape, large empty plastic bottle, hole punch, string, metal washer, pitcher, water

Water mills are built on the banks of rivers. Flowing water turns a waterwheel to create energy. The energy powers machines that do **physical** work. Waterwheels work much like **turbines** in water power plants.

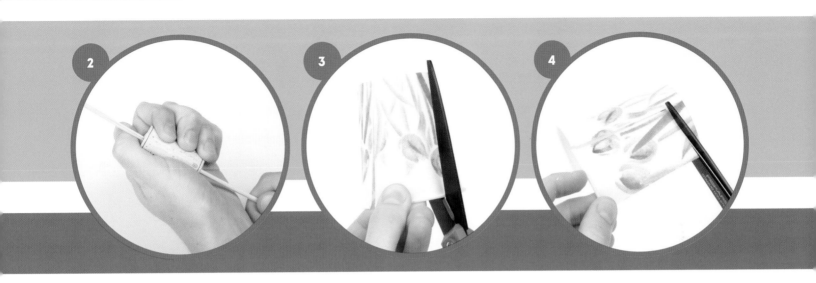

① Have an adult help you use a nail and hammer to make a hole lengthwise through the center of the cork.

② Push a wooden skewer through the hole in the cork. Push the cork to the center of the skewer.

③ Make six evenly spaced cuts around the cup. Cut from the cup's rim to the base. This divides the cup into six strips.

④ Cut the strips from the base of the cup.

Continued on the next page.

5 Trim each strip so it is the same length as the cork. Wrap duct tape around each strip. These are the blades of the waterwheel.

6 Duct tape the blades around the cork. Each blade should curve in the same direction. This is your waterwheel.

7 Cut the top off the plastic bottle.

8 Punch a hole near the top of the bottle. Punch a second hole across from the first.

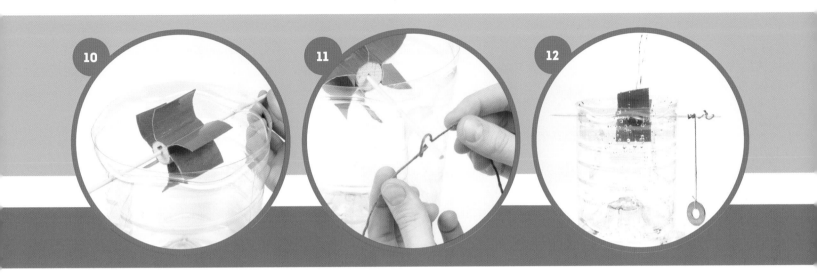

⑨ Slide the wooden skewer through the holes from the inside of the bottle.

⑩ Move the skewer until the waterwheel is in the center of the bottle.

⑪ Cut a piece of string that is a few inches longer than the bottle's height. Tie one end of the string to the washer. Tie the other end of the string to one end of the skewer.

⑫ Fill a pitcher with water. Slowly pour the water over the waterwheel into the bottle. The wheel causes the wooden skewer to turn. This lifts the washer off the ground!

WATER-POWERED BOAT

MATERIALS: Styrofoam cup, paint, paintbrush, craft foam, scissors, craft stick, hot glue gun & glue sticks, pencil, bendable drinking straw, small plastic lid, large aluminum pan, water, food coloring, spoon, liquid measuring cup

The force of gravity causes water to flow from high to low elevations. Flowing water has energy that can be used to do **physical** work. In this project, gravity pushes the water in the bottle downward. The energy of this downward current does the work of pushing the boat forward.

① Paint the cup. Let the paint dry.

② Cut a triangle out of craft foam. Glue it to the top of a craft stick for a sail. Glue the craft stick to the inside of the cup.

③ Use a pencil to poke a hole near the base of the cup.

④ Cut 2 to 3 inches (5 to 7.5 cm) off the long end of the straw. Push this end of the straw into the hole in the cup. Put hot glue around the straw to seal the hole.

⑤ Set the lid upside down on the table. Hot glue the cup to the center of the lid. Let the glue dry.

⑥ Put water in the pan. Add blue food coloring. Set the boat in the water. Bend the straw so the end is underwater.

⑦ Slowly pour water into the boat. The water will flow out through the straw and move the boat forward!

BUILD A DAM

MATERIALS: long plastic container, sand, pitcher, water, craft sticks, small rocks, blue food coloring, spoon

Dams can capture flowing water for use in water power plants. But not all dams were built for this purpose. Most dams were built to control flooding, water crops, or supply water to cities. Power plants are being added to many of these existing dams.

1. Fill the plastic container about halfway with sand.

2. Fill a pitcher with water. Pour water into the container until the sand is wet enough to shape.

3. Push some sand to one end of the container to create a hill.

Continued on the next page.

④ Dig a channel into the sand from the top of the hill to the bottom. This is your riverbed.

⑤ Push crafts sticks into the sand to build a dam at the bottom of the hill. Put rocks against each side of the dam to help hold it in place.

⑥ Fill the pitcher with water. Stir in a few drops of blue food coloring.

⑦ Slowly pour the water into the riverbed, starting at the top of the hill.

⑧ Watch what happens when the water reaches the dam. Does the dam break? Does the water form a pool behind the dam?

⑨ Experiment with different dam structures of rocks and craft sticks. Try pouring more or less water at a time. How do these changes affect how your dam works?

DIGGING DEEPER

Dams help turn water energy into clean, renewable power. However, they can also do harm. Dams can change river temperatures and water quality. This affects wildlife that live in the rivers. Dams also flood riverbanks. This destroys nearby **habitats**.

Dams can also keep fish from swimming up or downstream. Some dams use a fish ladder. This is a series of wide steps on the side of a dam. It lets fish swim around the dam. Experts are also working on building **turbines** that fish can safely swim through.

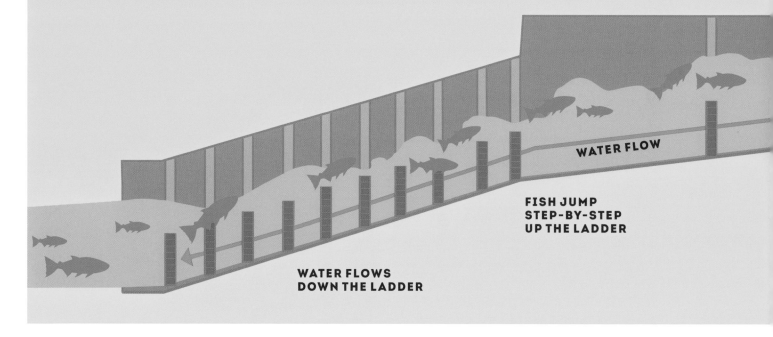

WATER FLOW

FISH JUMP
STEP-BY-STEP
UP THE LADDER

WATER FLOWS
DOWN THE LADDER

CONCLUSION

We get water energy from the force of moving water. It is a renewable **resource** fueled by the water **cycle**. Water power plants turn water energy into electricity. This electricity powers homes and businesses around the world!

QUIZ

1. What is electricity created with water energy called?

2. In a water power plant, what machine does water energy turn?

3. A Pelton waterwheel cup is not divided. TRUE OR FALSE?

LEARN MORE ABOUT IT!

You can find out more about water energy at the library. Or you can ask an adult to help you **research** water energy on the internet!

Answers: 1. Hydroelectricity 2. Turbine 3. False

GLOSSARY

condense – to change from a gas into a liquid or a solid. The liquid or solid formed is called condensation.

cycle – a series of events that happen over and over again.

divert – to change the direction or use of something. A change of direction is a diversion.

evaporate – to change from a liquid into a gas. This process is evaporation.

generator – a machine that creates electricity.

habitat – the area or environment where a person or animal usually lives.

irrigation – an act or process of supplying crops with water.

phase – a step or part in a series of events or actions.

physical – having to do with moving objects.

precipitation – moisture such as rain, hail, or snow that falls to Earth.

research – to find out more about something.

reservoir – a place where something is stored.

resource – something that is usable or valuable.

turbine – a machine that produces power when it is rotated at high speed.